THE CVLT OF WATER

THE OLD PAGAN GODS,
WHEN OUSTED BY CHRISTIANITY,
TOOK REFUGE IN THE RIVERS
WHERE THEY STILL DWELL.
OLD ENGLISH PROVERB

IF IT BE WISHED THAT ANY SUPERSTITION
SHOULD REMAIN AMONGST US,
IT IS THAT WHICH IS ATTACHED
A PECULIAR SACREDNESS TO THE PURE SPRING.
WE WOULD HAVE
ALL MEN WORSHIP WATER.
J SULLIVAN, MDCCCLXXIII

DAVID BRAMWELL & PETE FOWLER

ROUGH TRADE BOOKS x MUSEUM OF WITCHCRAFT AND MAGIC

THE
CULT
OF
WATER

It is said that the most powerful forces in society are revealed
by our tallest buildings.
Once our skylines were dominated by palaces, parliaments,
cathedrals and churches.
Now it is skyscrapers and office blocks.
Commerce is the ruling power, dwarfing the stone and spires
of the old gods.
But there are always exceptions.

When I'm eight years old my family trade the damp fens
of Lincolnshire for a Yorkshire town—Doncaster, Donny
or Danum as she was formerly known.
Once a key Roman settlement.
A gateway between north and south.
From my new bedroom window I can see houses and trees
but the skyline is dominated by two pale, concrete towers.
The tallest buildings for miles.
What mysterious beings inhabit these strange,
windowless monoliths?
I cycle out to them, stare up in wonder.
Unknown to me the most powerful force in my landscape
—*any* landscape—is water.

A few weeks later, deep in the woodland behind my new home—
binoculars in hand—I spy a little owl perched on the low branch
of a tree.
Birds are my latest obsession and I scour the ground on the
lookout for owl pellets.
There are none.
Instead I find an old blue teacup nestled in the undergrowth,
its handle long broken.
I am overwhelmed with a compulsion to take it to the towers.
I put the cup in my bag, cycle there and place it at the foot of
the taller of the two buildings.
An offering to whatever mysterious gods live there?
It was, I believe, my first act of worship.

All my life I've dreamed of water.
It's the same relentless nightmare that leaves me breathless
and terrified.
I'm in too deep, feet unable to find the bottom.
It's called thalassophobia—the primal fear of dark water,
of a creature that lurks in the murky depths with the power
to drag me down into madness and death.
And perhaps—if I have the courage to face it—the power to save.
I feel its presence in murky rivers, coastal waters and deep
mountain lakes.
'I am the spirit of dark and lonely waters,' whispered Donald Pleasance
in a terrifying 1970s public information film, warning children
of the perils of larking about near rivers.
It worked for me.
Too well.
But they did get one important detail wrong: the spirit of dark
and lonely water is female.

My family's move to Doncaster coincides with the great
heatwave of 1976.
England is in the grip of a drought.
Forest fires break out daily, temperatures hit 36 degrees.
The land is scorched and bleached.
With the heatwave come soaring numbers of aphids.
Hot on their trail—a plague of ladybirds.
Huge clouds of them shimmer through the air.
They stick in your hair and to your clothes.
Open your mouth for too long at your peril.
When the aphids have gone the ladybirds starve to death.
Millions of them litter the streets and countryside.
This was a biblical prophecy, English-style.

Something even stranger happens that summer.
In the midst of the heatwave we take a family trip to the
dark waters of Ladybower Reservoir in Derbyshire to see
the drowned church.
Building of the reservoir began in 1935, to provide water
to Manchester and surrounding towns.
Deep in the valley the villages of Derwent and Ashopton
were demolished.
Residents were ordered to leave their homes forever in the
name of progress.
Derwent's church held its last service in 1943.
But while the village was destroyed the church was left standing.
A mark of respect or superstition, perhaps?
And during times of severe drought, when the water levels
of Ladybower Reservoir fell sufficiently low, the church spire
would slowly re-emerge through the waters.

The Hillman Hunter parked up near Ladybower's dam; Mum, Dad, my sister and I bundle out and begin our walk to the water's edge. Within five minutes we're all dripping with sweat from the heat.
Ice lollies are procured and greedily consumed.
Standing in the shade, at the far end of the dam, we gaze out at the uncanny apparition of Derwent's belfry, like a stone creature rising from the depths.
A drowning god, coming up for air.
I was eight years old.
Some things, once seen, can never be forgotten.

It was the Don that, in 43AD, led the Romans to build a settlement at the lowest crossing of the river, a fort to divide north and south, and to keep out the fearsome Brigantes.
But the Don's legacy is older than the Romans.
Once she would have been venerated as a goddess.
To our ancestors, wells and springs were entrances to other worlds.
Rivers, lakes, lochs—each had their own guardians, deities, goddesses and nymphs.
The Romans named their new town Danum after Danu—
Celtic goddess of rivers, Hindu goddess of primordial waters.
Danu—the divine creator who birthed all things into being.
A hydromancer.

For those with the courage to sleep by her side she may divine
the future in her swirling eddies.
Danu, who gave her name to the Danube, the Duna, the Dane,
the Dunn, the Don.
Danu became Danum became Doncaster, a town built on
a river that has since forgotten its river.
An inconvenience it was shunted to the far side of the town,
neglected and unloved.
A river I grew up never knowing.
What happened to the Don, to Danu our river goddess?
What did we do to her?
Was there some mysterious connection between water and
the feminine?
Seeking answers, I paid a visit to England's greatest living wizard,
Alan Moore.

Over tea in his terraced Northampton home—'Sea View'—the
hirsute author and magician shared his thoughts on the symbolism
of water.

*'There's a fertility—a fecundity—to rivers, they bring life to the landscape.
In the East, undulant and natural lines like rivers are seen as the vectors
of good energy; straight lines are demonic. For the Chinese the dragon is an
auspicious symbol; it follows the shape of rivers and mountains. Here, since
the rise of Christianity at least, dragons are considered to be malevolent.
And, curiously, largely seen as female. It says something about the image
of St George spearing a dragon with his big, shiny lance.*

Throughout the world, water is largely seen as a female element. In the Tarot deck its corresponding suit is cups, which symbolises compassion. Of course male and female energies are both necessary for the creation of anything, whether that be an idea or whether that be a universe. If one of them is dominating however, that will lead to problems.'

One thing struck me after visiting the wizard, if male and female need to be in balance, didn't I need to see a witch? As you know, the North boasts more than its fair share of wise women.

I went to visit Anwen, a witch I knew living in the Peaks. She ran a shop, *Airy Fairy*, in Sheffield city centre and was unpacking a large box of scented candles when I arrived. I began by asking about Danu but found myself opening up about my fear of water, the nightmares, thalassophobia and this desire to re-connect with the Don.

She thought about it for a while then said,

'*Well, from a Jungian perspective, water is the classic symbol for the unconscious. If you're having water nightmares...hmmm... this is unresolved...*'

Anwen closed her eyes and thought a little while longer.

'*IT'S ABOUT VULCAN!*' she announced.

'Vulcan?'

Tutting, she marched me to the window.

'*Vulcan, there...do you see him? At the top of the tallest building?*'

In the distance I could see the statue of a man at the top of Sheffield Town Hall.

'*Roman god of fire and forge*', Anwen explained. '*Those are thunderbolts and a hammer in his hands. Sheffield's steel industry adopted him as their mascot. From a Pagan's point of view, he has a lot to answer for.*'
I was beginning to understand.
Like St George and the dragon, a great battle of the sexes had once taken place here—god of fire versus goddess of water.
Vulcan had been the victor.
The Don had been poisoned, left for dead.
'*You really want to understand Danu, re-connect with the river and be free of those nightmares?*' Anwen asked.
'*Yes*'.
'*Then you must take a journey back in time David, to the source of the*

Don. Pay your respects to Danu, make amends for Vulcan and face your fears. Will you do that?'
I nodded, unsure how. One of the witch's requests struck me as particularly tricky.
'Hang on, did you say "take a journey back in time to the source of the Don?"'
'Yes David, it must be a magical journey. To travel back in time you'll need to make an offering.'
'Erm—'
'Oh David, you'll know it when you see it,' she said and went back to wrestling with her giant box of candles.

If you'd been hanging out in Sheffield in the late seventies you might have chanced upon the unlikely scenario of a young Jarvis Cocker and friend floating through the city centre on an inflatable dingy.
Cocker was living in an area of Sheffield called Wicker at the time and the pair took to the waters, all the way to Rotherham. Parts of the journey he describes as 'evil-smelling and stagnant'. He also speaks fondly of this as one of the happiest days in his life and immortalised the journey on the Pulp album *Life*, with the song *Wickerman*.

Just behind the station, before you reach the traffic island, a river runs through a concrete channel.
I took you there once; I think it was after the Leadmill.
The water was dirty and smelt of industrialisation
Little mesters coughing their lungs up and globules the colour of tomato ketchup.
But it flows. Yeah, it flows.

Underneath the city through dirty brickwork conduits
Connecting white witches on the Moor with pre-raphaelites
down in Broomhall.
Beneath the old Trebor factory that burnt down in the early seventies.
Leaving an antiquated sweet-shop smell and caverns of nougat and caramel.
Nougat. Yeah, nougat and caramel.
And the river flows on.

Cocker's happiness of letting the river take him is echoed
in Tom Fort's book *Downstream*.
In 2008 the journalist took a solitary trip by punt down the Trent.
Fort got as far as the Trent Aegir—a tidal bore—then got out and
cycled the rest of the way to the sea as it was too treacherous.
'Looking back, my days on the Trent were some of the happiest in my life,'
Fort said in an interview.

In East Sussex, during the noughties, author Olivia Laing walked
the forty-two miles of the River Ouse from source to sea.
The end of a long relationship had left her feeling displaced.
'I wanted to recover some sense of home,' she said and recorded the
walk in her book, *To the River.*
The ghost of Virginia Woolf haunts its pages.
This was the same river that, seventy years previously, Woolf
had walked to one morning, her pockets full of stones.
In a suicide note Woolf wrote, *'I am doing what seems to be the
best thing to do.'*
Laing's pilgrimage down the Ouse however was cleansing
and cathartic.
She returned home refreshed from the experience.
But Fort, Laing and Cocker had all travelled *downstream*, going
with the flow, like Huckleberry Finn on the Mississippi.

On the witch's insistence, I would be walking from Doncaster, following the river to Sheffield and into the wilds of the Pennines to Loxley, Oughtibridge, Scout Dike and beyond.

I was to be heading inland, travelling *against* the flow, like Marlow penetrating the Congo in search of Kurtz, a dark journey of the soul that would challenge his faith in so-called civilised man. Would I too be heading into the heart of darkness?

◆

I leave my parents' house early in the morning, the water towers just visible through the haze.

Past the Danum retail outlet, down Scot Lane, Goose Hill, Baxter Gate.

The pungent odour of the fish vendors, the shrill cry of the market traders.

Down Balby Road, where William Senior's Sand House once stood.

A subterranean folly, its tunnels sculpted with exotic creatures and lined with giant fungi.

A delight for all visitors.

Until 1935, when the council could see no further use for it and filled it with concrete.

Past Frenchgate, formerly The Arndale Centre where, in 1967, Eckehart Selke's statue *The Lovers* was erected.

A golden naked couple joined at the hips.

Male and female united.

Arms aloft in the throes of ecstasy.

A glorious and endless fuck, right in the middle of Doncaster's busy new shopping centre.

Until 1988 when, amidst growing concerns that someone might take offence, *The Lovers* was removed.

I keep walking.
Over the North Bridge and there she lay—the Don.
Descending her banks I slip and nearly tumble into
her dark waters.
Picking myself up my keen birder's eye is drawn to a post,
fifty yards to my left.
Senatorial, a little owl stands upright, feathers ruffled
in the slight breeze.
Instinctively I look down.
Astonished.
There at my feet—that old blue teacup, its handle long broken.
I pick it up, clean it and cast it into the Don's waters.
An offering.
And I am back in the summer of 1976.

Hit by the blistering heat I begin to walk.
Past the prison to Sprotbrough, Denaby Main and Conisbrough.
House martins chatter.
Clouds of ladybirds swirl around my head.
I fan my face to keep them away.
They cling to my clothes and bury themselves in my hair.
The heat subsides and I am walking back through the decades
to the 1920s.
Canalised, manipulated and poisoned by industry, the Don
oozes through a broken landscape.
A forgotten river.
A stinking cesspool.
It is heartbreaking to witness.
I cover my nose with a hankie and trudge on.
And time rolls back.

Choked by the coal industry at Mexborough, polluted from the heavy steelworks of Rotherham and Sheffield, the Don is diverted to soothe Vulcan's hellish heat.

In the distance is the Templeborough steelworks.

Half a kilometre in length, it is the largest electric melting shop in the world.

Controlling it all from the tallest building in the city—the town hall—I spy him.

Hammer in one hand, thunderbolts in the other.

Vulcan, holding forth over his empire.

Danu his captor.

The Don is imprisoned behind high walls now, inaccessible to me.

Poisoned and slowly dying.

In 1890 across the Atlantic, William James—the father of American psychology—coins the phrase, 'stream of consciousness'.

It occurs to him that our thoughts flow like water.

And like water they are without form, yet responsible for creating form.

It has occurred to others too.

In 1797 Samuel Taylor Coleridge drops in on his friend Wordsworth in Dorset for a few days.

Days become weeks. The pair finally head off to walk the Quantocks together, conceiving an epic river poem as the perfect metaphor for our inner and outer worlds and the circular nature of the spiritual life.

But Coleridge could be a difficult bugger at times.

The two men fall out before committing pen to paper.

That same year however, inspired by an opium-soaked dream, Coleridge begins to write *Kubla Khan*, in which the sacred River Alph—a mighty force—surges up like a huge fountain.

Until he is interrupted by the infamous visitor from Porlock.

In western psychology we have Flow Theory.
When we are energised, creative, directed and happy
we are 'in the flow'.
It is hardly a new idea.
Over two millennia ago the Chinese developed Taoism—the way,
harmony, going with the flow.
Exemplified—according to one book at least—by Winnie the Pooh.

A form of occupational therapy in Japan is called *The Kawa River Model*, which compares the three stages of a river to our own stages of life.
The juvenile river is powerful, clear and fast-moving but lacking in depth.
By middle-age it has slowed and deepened.
It is also beginning to gather sediment.
'Baggage'.
It is broadening too, becoming a little generous around the midriff.
By old age the river is wide, slow and serpentine.
It has great depth.
And a wealth of life in and around it.
It is also prone to being blocked, diverted, dried out, silted up.
Work out what's blocking your flow and you may find resolution.

But as a river reaches the sea does it really end there?
The river is both linear and cyclical.
With a river we are bearing witness to past, present
and future simultaneously.

I continue my journey along the Don back through the centuries.
The Industrial Revolution is yet to be.
The air is clean, sky swollen with clouds of starlings.

Skylarks trill overhead and parachute into long grass.
The Don is flowing, thriving, pregnant with fish.
It is so abundant with salmon that they are considered
to be the food of paupers.
The rich dine out on the lamprey, carp, bream and perch
that also breed in her crystal-clear waters.
Ahead of me I witness a tragedy in the making.
Carpenter Robert Leche and his family attempt to cross
a ford but their wagon is swept away, drowning the horse
and pulling them under.
I watch, horrified.
Those nearby cry out for a miracle to save them.
Their prayers are answered.
Leche and family make it safely to the riverbank.
Five hundred years later a shrine to Our Lady of Doncaster
will stand in the church of St Peter-in-Chains on Chequer Road.
With the power to save.

Danu?

I walk another mile and into the late fifteenth century.
On the outskirts of Sheffield near the confluence of the Don
and the Rother is the chapel-on-the-bridge, a chantry.
It is one of only a few purpose-built places of Christian worship
to sit directly over a river.
In less than 60 years the Reformation will lead to its closure.
Over the centuries this chantry will become the unlikely location
for Rotherham's jail, a tobacconist and—for a while—home to local
resident John Watson.
The scorch marks from his fire can still be seen on the east wall.
But the chantry was really built as a spiritual safeguard for
travellers like myself, journeying in and out of town on the only
road over the river.

It is dusk as I approach.
A monk with a lighted candle sits high up in an alcove—
an invitation to pay my respect with a toll.
An offering.
Our pre-Christian ancestors would once have thrown coins
in the river to appease the goddess.
It is a ritual that continues to this day, every time we drop
a coin down a well for good luck.

A few miles on I walk quickly through the dirt roads of
a small, insignificant market town called Sheffield, up one
of its seven hills and back into 950AD.
The church is having difficulty suppressing its subjects'
desires to worship water.
So King Edgar passes a law to extinguish Paganism.
No man may attribute reverence or sanctity to a well,
river or spring without the Bishop's authority.
This is meant to be a Christian island now, after all.

As I leave Sheffield for the heathland the air gets chilly.
I turn up my coat collar, stuff hands in pockets and begin
my ascent.
I climb with the Don on the outskirts of the Pennines.
Dippers bob downstream.
Flocks of brambling and goldfinch chatter overhead.
I am in the first millennium.
Christianity is being peddled to an island of heathens.
But myths and rituals are traded, interwoven.
Churches are built on the sites of holy wells and springs
and rededicated in honour of a Christian saint.
We worship Jesus the fisherman.

We baptise the newborn by sprinkling them with spring
water and immersing converts in a sacred river.
This isn't learned from some holy book but a ritual taught
to us long ago by Norsemen and Teutons.
We tell stories of how the holy ghost emerged from the depths
of a sacred well to impregnate Mary.
Not the Virgin Mary but Mary the Great Fish.
Our lady, star of the sea: Stella Maris.
Mary, from Sumerian *Mar*—the ocean.
Mary, from whose name we get maritime, marriage, ma.
And nightmare.
Where she transforms into a fearful creature from the depths—
the spirit of dark and lonely water.
Approach with caution.
She has the power to save and show you the future.
Or pull you under, to madness and death.

And I am in the wilds of the Pennines now, the rule
of Constantine 300AD.
There is snow underfoot.
Bodies of water are entrances to other worlds.
Often to the land of the dead.
The Romans cast their shields, helmets and coins
into our rivers as votive offerings.
They worship the thermal waters at Buxton.
At Bath their goddess Minerva unites with the Celtic
goddess Sulis and a cult is formed.
Coins for healing and sheets of lead with curses inscribed
are thrown into the warm waters of the spring.
But even the Roman Empire is yet to be as I reach the final
leg of my journey and enter a cold, Neolithic realm.

The Don is just a stream.
I have arrived in a Pagan place—a moorland of heather, bracken
and moss where springs and wells are gateways, each with their
own nymphs and deities.
We drive nails into trees and tie rags on branches as an act
of ceremonial union with the goddess.
It is not churches erected by her side now but standing stones.
Male and female united.

The monolith and the well.

                                        The line and the circle.

The sword and the chalice.

                                        The line and the circle.

The Spear of Destiny and the Holy Grail.

                                        The line and the circle.

The male and female sexual organs.

                                        The line and the circle.

From the Cerne Giant to CERN.

                                        The line and the circle.

Linear and cyclical time.

                                        The line and the circle.

Binary code.

                                        The line and the circle.

Millennia from now, endless data streams of ones and zeros
will drive a new mythic, digital realm.
Here, past present and future are connected by time's arrow
and time's circle.
And I have reached the source of the Don.
Before me is a dream palace, an oracle.
I approach Danu for guidance and offer her coins from my pocket.
I drink her water.
It has been a long journey.

I have walked forty miles and travelled for thousands of years.
Tired, I fall into a deep sleep.

✳

In *Finnegans Wake*, author James Joyce opens with the
word, 'riverrun'.
Dublin's river Liffey leads us into the narrative, into the
city and runs through the whole book.
Joyce imagines the city and its buildings as masculine,
the Liffey as feminine.

*'Riverrun, past Eve and Adams, from swerve of shore to bend of bay,
brings us by a commodious vicus of recirculation back to Howth Castle
and Environs.'*

The final page returns us to the sea and returns to the
opening lines.

*'A way a lone, a lost, a last, a loved along the riverrun, past Eve and
Adams, from swerve of shore to bend of bay...'*

Finnegans Wake never ends but, like a river, is a re-circulation,
starting and ending with the same sentence.
But it is never the same.
You may never step into the same *Finnegans Wake* twice.
For while the words never change, you do.
When Joyce wrote *Finnegans Wake* he no longer believed
he was simply writing a book but performing a work of magic.
Though it could be argued that all art is a work of magic.

✳

And in the night she comes.
I'm back again in that familiar nightmare, alone in an
endless body of water, gripped by loneliness and terror.
Below—ominous shapes, the fear of what lies beneath.
The lingering shadow of madness and death.
The spirit of dark and lonely water.
Waiting to drag me under.

I am the drowned village.
I am the church spire.
I am the Christian god gasping for air.
I am the villagers engulfed by water, drowned by progress.
I am Vulcan the patriarch.
I am...

...pulled under.

Fighting for air I feel my lungs burning, hands flailing.
Panic-stricken I become entangled in weeds.
Weeds become hair, the long green tendrils of the goddess.
She is Danu, Peg Powler, Coventina, Jenny Greenteeth, Peg O'Nell.
The goddess sits on a throne of reeds in the depths of every great
body of water, possessing soul and will.
She is a supernatural creature that lurks in the dark, exerting
her power over life itself.
And I am drowning in her.

All is darkness as I finally surrender.
I am entwined in her serpentine body, her flowing hair,
her round lips.
The battle is over.

And there is a taste in my mouth.
It is the taste of the goddess.
Not death or madness.
It is the taste of compassion.

*'I'm pretty good at divining the sex of unborn babies by a method taught
to me by my mother, which involves a needle and thread. What you do
is take the thread and let the needle hang suspended over the pregnant
women's bulge. If the needle starts to move in a circle then it'll be a
daughter. If it starts to swing back and forth it'll be a boy.'*

Alan Moore

I wake from my slumbers to the cry of a buzzard circling overhead.
The snow has gone.
Sun warms my skin.
Hungry I walk though the centuries, across the Pennines, away
from the Don and into Derbyshire.
Ladybirds litter the roadside.
I am back again in the summer of 1976.
I reach Ladybower Reservoir and look out across its low waters.
But there is no sign of the drowned church.
Where is it?

Scrambling down the coiled dragon lines of Winnats Pass
I reach the village of Castleton and the present.
Drawn by food and shelter.
A pie and a pint in a dusty old pub—northern alchemy.
With food and beer in my belly I explore the town, following

a stream-side path to the Devil's Arse Cavern, former home
to a village of rope-makers.
At a nearby vintage emporium a purchase is made—an old book,
Silent Valley, detailing the history of LadyBower Reservoir.
I have photos of Derwent's drowned church in my house.
It has been my screen saver.
I have used it as a cover image for an album.
Friends have made me artwork of it.
It has remained an obsession.

Written and researched by Valerie Hallam, *Silent Valley* contains
photos and accounts of that extraordinary event.
But where are the pictures from the summer our family visited—
the heatwave of 1976?
Within its pages I make a new discovery.
Three decades previously—in 1947—an earlier drought had
brought such an unwelcome volume of sightseers and divers that
the church had been demolished to curb further intrusions.
In 1976 there *was* no church rising from those dark waters.
It wasn't there.
When I mention this later to my family at first there is silence.
Then my dad says firmly, '*I remember.*'
And we all do.
We're not alone; others saw it too.
In the blistering heat of that summer were we party to a mirage,
a mass hallucination?

Like the phantom limb of an amputee, is Derwent's church locked
in the memory of those dark and lonely waters?
Or was it a prophecy perhaps—a vision—that one day, in an act
of compassion, our god of fire and brimstone might again feel the
embrace of an old lover?
Male and female re-united.

It is March 2011, the night of a full moon.
At the edge of St Helen's Wood in Hastings, East Sussex,
Mark Golding blesses two doses of LSD and swallows them
with a glass of water.
He does this to face new fear.
Fear for the life of his son, Gus, struck by a debilitating illness
during a holiday in Thailand.
Gus's infected lungs have left him suspended between this
world and the next.
The story reaches out to a nation and, through a tabloid
newspaper campaign, money is raised to bring him home.
But Gus is critically ill.
Mark feels helpless, afraid.
His solution?
To drop acid and ask the spirits of the woodlands and
waterways for help.
Well, he is an old hippie after all.

Mark surrenders to the darkness of the ancient Sussex
woodland and its network of streams.
Soon he is up to his knees in fresh running water, bent in
the undergrowth, working until his hands are frozen,
clothes soaked, in certain knowledge that this complex
of streams and tributaries are actually Gus's damaged lungs.

In removing debris from the water Mark is purifying
his son's failing organs.
But the blockages are endless—miles of tributaries,
their flow inhibited.
Illuminated with LSD, Mark turns to the water goddess for help.
Her message is clear.
Find the source.
Purify and cleanse the epicentre.
Remove the blockage and Gus will live.

An old Ordnance Survey map reveals the location of the spring.
It is a foul smelling, fetid place, unvisited for years.
Mark plunges his bare hands into its waters.
Belching and sliming, its water content vomits from a long-lost
hidden outlet.
For days Mark works without rest.
Then, into the compacted earth and debris, he finds a slab.
Then another.
It is beginning to look like a man-made channel.
Over the next few days Mark clears the channel and
discovers a pool.
Digging down reveals its circular form, constructed
from old, smooth rocks.
It is large enough to bathe in.
To be fully immersed.
Mark drinks the water to taste its qualities and learn its mysteries.
Suddenly he is aware of an enormous cruciform oak to the rear
of the spring and, to the right, a giant ancient beech tree.
Carved into the tree—*alchemy*.
This has long been a place of worship.
Behind the beech tree a short pathway once led to an old Hastings
boarding house—*Netherwood*, resting home of 'The Great Beast',
Aleister Crowley.
Make of that what you will.

Mark begins to invite friends to the spring, to help
in its restoration, to bathe, and for rites and rituals.
He takes water from the spring to his son each week.
After a year the chest drain is removed from Gus's lung cavity.
He's going to be alright.
Though for Gus, at least, the doctors and their medicine played
their part too.

Once we gazed into fires and rivers to stir our imaginations.
Now we stare into screens, tormented by the faint memory
of a lover we cannot place.
But we mustn't give up the search.
There are those who she still calls upon.
An echo of her voice is enough.
In the small hours they slip out alone, unaware of the task
that they have been given, an army of solitary guardians,
sitting in silent worship on the banks of her soothing waters.
Fishing rods—divining rods—in hand.

In our cities and towns, rivers and waterways are being cleaned
up and made accessible to us again.
And we are drawn—to live, to sleep, to walk, to meditate,
to go with the flow.
We are an island of water-worshippers after all.
Vulcan's empire has crumbled.
The Templeborough steelworks is now Magna, a science
adventure centre.
In Doncaster, Eckehart Selke's controversial statue, *The Lovers,*
has been restored and resurrected atop a glass podium in a quieter
part of the town.

Plans are afoot for it be returned to its rightful place
in the heart of Doncaster's busy shopping centre.
The Don is on the mend.
In Sheffield city centre salmon passes can be found.
The fish are returning.
Red deer take to the river at night.
Our lover is returning.
But we must remain vigilant.
2019 saw some of the worst flooding for decades along the Don.
Warnings went unheeded.
Houses and villages were drowned.
She has the power to save.
And the power to drag us under if not treated with the
reverence she deserves.

Down by the sprawling shopping centre of Meadowhall,
on the outskirts of Sheffield, growing unnoticed by the
banks of the Don are fig trees.
The Don's waters, once polluted and heated, flowed with
the sewage of Vulcan's men.
But germinating in their digestive tracts and in those heated waters
were seeds from the fig biscuits favoured by the factory workers.
Now a fig forest.
Sweet, delicious fruit.
A new Garden of Eden by the banks of the Don.
We have come full circle.
Cast your swords, coins and shields into her waters boys,
we still have far to go.

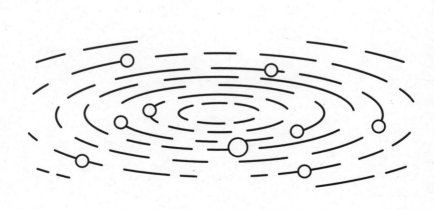

DAVID BRAMWELL

DAVID BRAMWELL IS SINGER-SONGWRITER IN ODDFELLOW'S CASINO, AUTHOR OF 'THE N09 BUS TO UTOPIA' AND 'THE HAUNTED MOUSTACHE' AND A SONY AWARD-WINNING BROADCASTER. FOR BBC R3 AND BBC R4 HE HAS MADE PROGRAMMES ON SUBJECTS RANGING FROM IVOR CUTLER AND KEN CAMPBELL TO TIME TRAVEL.

'THE CULT OF WATER' BEGAN LIFE AS AN EXPERIMENTAL RADIO PROGRAMME FOR BBC R3'S BETWEEN THE EARS, AND AS A LIVE MULTIMEDIA SHOW, MIXING ARCHIVE FOOTAGE, SPOKEN WORD, MUSIC AND RITUAL. IT IS AVAILABLE AS A LIVE ALBUM COMBINING MUSIC, NARRATIVE AND THE MIGHTY VOICE OF ALAN MOORE.

WWW.DRBRAMWELL.COM @DRBRAMWELL

I I

I

PETE FOWLER IS AN ARTIST, DESIGNER, DJ AND MUSICIAN. HE IS ONE-HALF OF THE BAND SEAHAWKS AND HAS CREATED ALBUM COVERS FOR SUPER FURRY ANIMALS AND ARTWORK FOR BANDS INCLUDING THE HORRORS AND TIM BURGESS. HIS ILLUSTRATIONS ADORN BOOK COVERS, T-SHIRTS, SKATEBOARDS, COMICS AND PRINTS. HE HAS SPENT SEVERAL YEARS CREATING MONSTERS.

PETE FOWLER

III

AIDED BY A WITCH AND THE MAGICIAN ALAN MOORE, DAVID BRAMWELL TAKES AN OCCULT JOURNEY BACK IN TIME UP THE RIVER DON, IN SEARCH OF THE SUPERNATURAL SECRETS OF OUR WATERWAYS AND TO SOLVE THE MYSTERY OF A DROWNED VILLAGE WHICH HAS LONG HAUNTED HIS MEMORIES. TRAVELLING THROUGH THE INDUSTRIAL DESTRUCTION OF OUR LANDSCAPE HE ARRIVES IN A PRE-CHRISTIAN ERA WHEN WELLS AND SPRINGS WERE WORSHIPPED AS LIVING DEITIES, BRINGING HIM FACE TO FACE WITH DANU, THE GODDESS OF PRIMORDIAL WATERS. CAN BRAMWELL FACE HIS DEMONS AND UNRAVEL THE SYMBOLIC MYSTERIES OF OUR ANCIENT ANCESTORS? WHO IS THE MYSTERIOUS VULCAN? AND WILL THERE BE A PIE AND A PINT WAITING FOR HIM AT THE END OF IT ALL?

Published in association with the Museum of Witchcraft and Magic, these special Rough Trade Editions seek dialogue with the culture and folklore of magical practice. Through hallucinatory fiction, illustration, a deeply personal essay and the fates, a range of artists collaborated to create new works that take their shape from the fascinating, alternative history of the museum.

ROUGH TRADE BOOKS

MUSEUM OF WITCHCRAFT AND MAGIC

9	7	8	–
1	–	9	1
2	7	2	2
–	7	2	3

ISBN 978-1-912722-72-3

9 781912 722723